UKRAINE

UKRAINE

THEN & NOW

Prepared by
Geography Department

Lerner Publications Company
Minneapolis

Series editors: Mary M. Rodgers, Tom Streissguth,
  Colleen Sexton
Photo researcher: Bill Kauffmann
Designer: Zachary Marell

Our thanks to the following people for their help in
preparing and checking the text of this book: Dr. Craig
ZumBrunnen, Department of Geography, University of
Washington; Slavko Nowytski; and Dr. Anatol and Mrs.
Daria Lysyj.

Pronunciation Guide

Bohdan	bo-HDAAN
Khmelnytskyi	hmell-NYIT-skee
Dnepropetrovsk	dnye-pro-peht-ROFSK
Dnieper	DNEE-per
Dniester	DNEE-ster
glasnost	GLAZ-nost
hryvnia	HRIV-nyah
Mykhailo	mih-HY-lo
Hrushevsky	hroo-SHEV-skee
perestroika	pehr-eh-STROY-kah
Pereiaslav	pehr-ay-eh-SLAV
Rukh	ROOH
sukhovey	soo-hoh-VEE

Terms in **bold** are listed in a glossary that starts on page 60.

LIBRARY OF CONGRESS CATALOGING-IN-PUBLICATION DATA

Ukraine/prepared by Geography Department, Lerner Publica-
tions Company.
    p.   cm.—(Then & Now)
    Includes index.
    Summary: Examines the history, geography, ethnic mixture,
politics, economy, and future of the former Soviet republic of
Ukraine.
    ISBN 0-8225-2808-8 (lib. bdg.)
    1. Ukraine—Juvenile literature. [1. Ukraine.] I. Lerner
Publications Company. Geography Dept. II. Series: Then & Now
(Minneapolis, Minn.)
DK508.12.U37 1992
947'.71—dc20   92-10284
                                                   CIP
                                                   AC

Manufactured in the United States of America
2 3 4 5 6 – I/JR – 98 97 96 95 94 93

• CONTENTS •

A costumed member of Kiev's Shevchenko Opera and Ballet Theater waits to go on stage. Kiev has been the cultural and political capital of Ukraine since the 9th century.

"The Soviet Union has disintegrated. An independent Ukraine is born."
Leonid Kravchuk

In 1992, the Soviet Union would have celebrated the 75th anniversary of the revolution of 1917. During that revolt, political activists called **Communists** overthrew the czar (ruler) and the government of the **Russian Empire.** The revolution of 1917 was the first step in establishing the 15-member **Union of Soviet Socialist Republics (USSR)**, which included the republics of Russia and Ukraine.

The Soviet Union stretched from eastern Europe across northern Asia and contained nearly 300 million people. Within this vast nation, the Communist government guaranteed housing, education, health care, and lifetime employment. Communist leaders told farmers and factory workers that Soviet citizens owned all property in common. The new nation quickly **industrialized**, meaning it built many new factories and upgraded existing ones. It also modernized and enlarged its farms. In addition, the USSR created a huge, well-equipped military force that allowed it to become one of the most powerful nations in the world.

Ukrainians displayed political banners and blue-and-yellow Ukrainian flags on August 24, 1991 — the day that the country declared its independence from Soviet rule.

Ukraine, one of the largest and most populous republics within the Soviet Union, provided the USSR with much of its food, many raw materials and minerals, and substantial industrial goods. The first Slavic state arose in Ukraine more than 1,000 years ago, and the country has close ties with **Slavs** in Russia. Nevertheless, the Ukrainian people have maintained their separate language and culture and have fought for independence throughout the 20th century.

By the late 1980s, the Soviet Union was in a period of rapid change and turmoil. The central government had mismanaged the economy, which was failing to provide goods. People throughout the vast nation were dissatisfied. The widespread movement for independence among the Soviet republics worried some old-style Communist leaders.

A poster from 1991 shows Soviet president Mikhail Gorbachev trapped in a vessel on a rocky sea. The quote in Russian reads "Don't rock the boat."

НЕ РАСКАЧИВАЙТЕ МНЕ ЛОДКУ!

Flowers and ribbons decorate a street memorial to Taras Shevchenko, Ukraine's most famous poet. Born a serf in 1814, Shevchenko gained his freedom in 1838 and eventually became a university professor in Kiev. His writings—all in the Ukrainian language—sparked nationalist feelings among Ukrainians living under Russian rule.

Demonstrators shouted their opposition to the attempted overthrow of Gorbachev by conservative Communists in August 1991.

In the summer of 1991, Soviet president Mikhail Gorbachev proposed a treaty that would allow the Soviet republics more economic and political freedom. In response, conservative Communists tried to overthrow Gorbachev in a violent **coup d'état**.

Although the coup failed, Ukrainians later voted for independence from the Soviet Union, an action that hastened the breakup of the USSR. The republic's leaders moved to create a Ukrainian army and a separate Ukrainian currency. In December 1991, the leaders of Ukraine and other Soviet republics formed the **Commonwealth of Independent States.** This loose association is trying to establish common trade and defense policies. Since declaring independence, Ukraine has been recognized by Russia and by many other countries of the world as a sovereign nation.

CHAPTER ONE

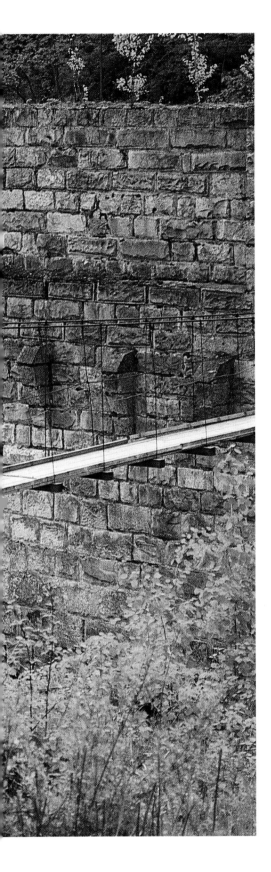

The Land and People of Ukraine

Ukraine lies north of the Black Sea in south-eastern Europe. With an area of 233,089 square miles (603,700 square kilometers), the country is slightly smaller than the state of Texas and is larger than France. Romania and the former Soviet republic of Moldova sit southwest of Ukraine. Hungary and Slovakia share short frontiers to the west. Belarus—the former Soviet republic of Byelorussia—and Poland lie to the north and northwest, respectively. Ukraine's long eastern border with Russia runs from Belarus southward to the Sea of Azov, an arm of the Black Sea.

Near the city of Kosov in western Ukraine, hikers trek across the Prut River. The river rises in the Carpathian Mountains and crosses the Ukrainian border into nearby Romania and Moldova.

The Dnieper, Europe's third longest river, flows through several large Ukrainian cities, including Kiev, Dnepropetrovsk, and Kherson. Navigable for most of its length, the waterway also provides hydroelectric power to these industrial hubs.

The name *Ukraine* comes from a Slavic word meaning "borderland." Throughout its history, Ukraine has been a gateway for travelers moving eastward to Asia, as well as an important route westward into Europe. The region also formed the westernmost territory of the old Russian Empire.

Ukrainians are changing the names of their cities and regions to reflect the Ukrainian language and pronunciation. The capital city of Kiev, for example, is becoming widely known as Kyiv. Nevertheless, Ukraine remains closely tied to Russia and to the eastern European nations that have, at various times, claimed Ukrainian lands and influenced Ukrainian culture.

• Topography and Rivers •

Most of Ukraine's territory is made up of level, fertile plains known as **steppes.** Elevations on the steppes are greatest in the north and west and grad-

Ukraine's fertile soil enables farmers to grow a wide variety of crops, including wheat, corn, rye, potatoes, and flax.

ually decrease near the coast of the Black Sea. A section of rolling steppes in northeastern Ukraine continues into Russia. Along Ukraine's northern border with Belarus are the sandy Pripet Marshes, where settlement is sparse. A belt of lowlands, lying below 200 feet (61 meters), extends from the Pripet Marshes into northeastern Ukraine.

Three major rivers—the Dniester, Dnieper, and Donets—flow through Ukraine. The wide Dnieper River crosses into Ukraine from Belarus and winds through a broad, flat plain before reaching its outlet near the southern city of Kherson. To the west of the Dnieper are the Volhyn Uplands, which reach a maximum elevation of 1,514 feet (461 m). The Dniester and Southern Bug (Boh) rivers and their tributaries cross the Volhyn-Podolsk region in western Ukraine, dividing the area's high plateaus into a series of river valleys.

In central and southern Ukraine, the Dnieper River flows through dams and artificial lakes that generate hydroelectric power. This area's fertile plains and its rich black soil—called **chornozem**—have made Ukraine one of the most productive agricultural regions in Europe. Southeast of the lower Dnieper valley are the Azov Heights, a series of irregular hills that reach about 1,000 feet (305 m). These uplands descend to the northern coast of the Sea of Azov.

In the southwestern corner of Ukraine rises a spur of the Carpathian Mountains, which continue southeastward into Romania. Hoverla, the highest point in the Ukrainian Carpathians, reaches 6,762 feet (2,061 m). The Crimean Peninsula, which juts into the Black Sea from southern Ukraine, has a long and irregular coastline with many small bays, lagoons, and sandy lowlands. The Crimean Mountains, which reach 5,068 feet (1,545 m), rise abruptly along the peninsula's southern coast.

Sunbathers crowd a beach in Crimea, a large, irregularly shaped peninsula on the coast of the Black Sea. Although the peninsula has no physical connection to Russia, Crimea once belonged to Russia and still has a Russian majority. In 1954, the Soviet government made Crimea part of Ukraine in honor of Russian-Ukrainian unity. In May 1992, Crimeans voted for self-rule, a move that the Ukrainian government denied.

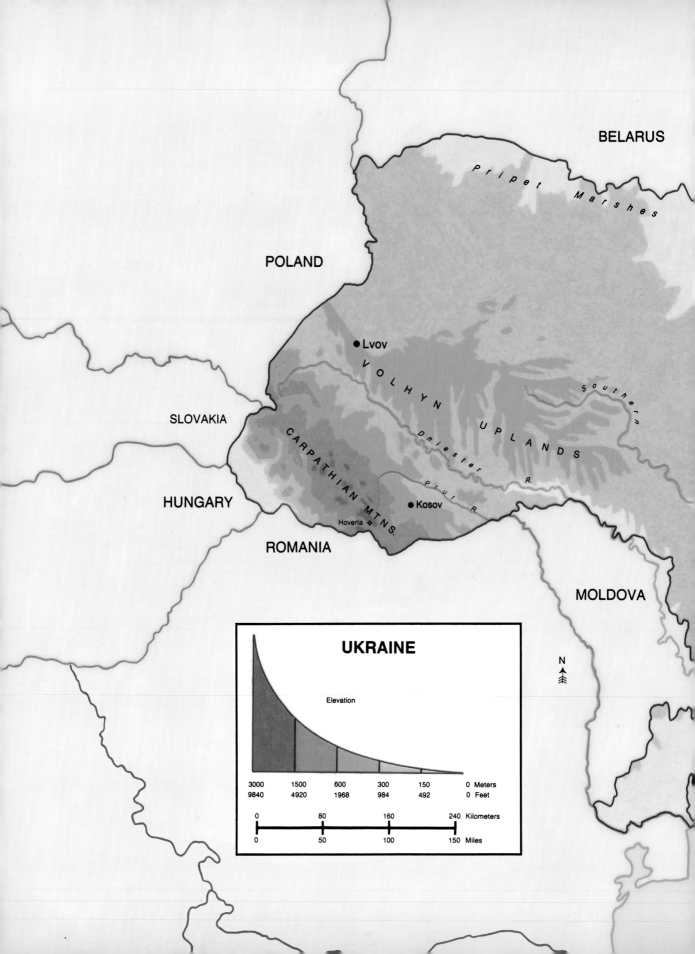

BELARUS

Pripet Marshes

POLAND

● Lvov

V O L H Y N

Southern

SLOVAKIA

C A R P A T H I A N   M T N S.

Dniester

R.

Prut R.

U P L A N D S

HUNGARY

● Kosov

Hoverla ◇

ROMANIA

MOLDOVA

UKRAINE

Elevation

| 3000 | 1500 | 600 | 300 | 150 | 0 Meters |
| 9840 | 4920 | 1968 | 984 | 492 | 0 Feet |

N

| 0 | | 80 | | 160 | | 240 Kilometers |
| 0 | 50 | | 100 | | 150 Miles |

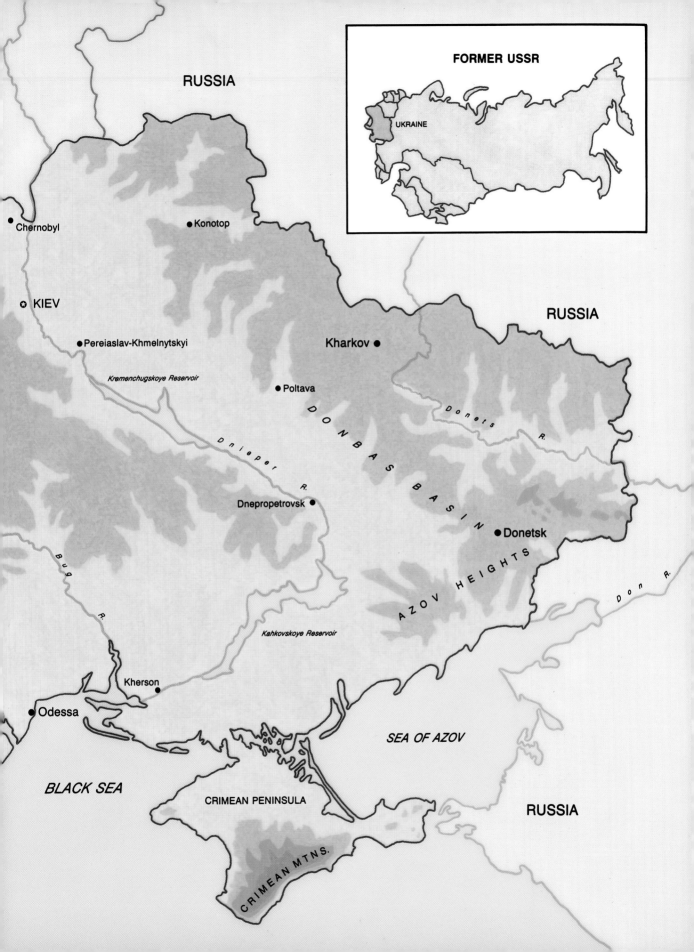

FORMER USSR

UKRAINE

RUSSIA

RUSSIA

RUSSIA

• Chernobyl

• Konotop

✪ KIEV

• Pereiaslav-Khmelnytskyi

Kharkov •

Kremenchugskoye Reservoir

• Poltava

D O N B A S   B A S I N

Dnieper   R.

Donets   R.

Dnepropetrovsk •

• Donetsk

B u g   R.

A Z O V   H E I G H T S

Kahkovskoye Reservoir

Don   R.

• Kherson

• Odessa

SEA OF AZOV

BLACK SEA

CRIMEAN PENINSULA

CRIMEAN MTNS.

• *Climate* •

Most of Ukraine experiences warm summers and cold winters. Average January temperatures range from 28° F (–2° C) in the southwest to 18° F (–8° C) in the northeast. Kiev averages 21° F (–6° C) in January, the coldest month, and 67° F (19°C) in July, the warmest month. Throughout most of the country, snow covers the ground for about three months during the winter.

Rainfall during the summer is heaviest in the northwest, where the average annual precipitation is 24 inches (61 centimeters). More than 31 inches (80 cm) of rain and snow fall in the Carpathian Mountains.

Citizens in Lvov, a large city in western Ukraine, keep their umbrellas handy during an autumn rainstorm.

Snow dusts a flower display in front of Lvov's Ivan Franko University.

A sign in Ukrainian advertises tasty and healthful fruit juices to thirsty citizens in the capital.

Summer storms interrupt long periods of warm and dry weather throughout the country. July temperatures average about 70° F (21° C). Hot, dry winds known as **sukhoviyi** blow from the east in the summer, causing occasional droughts. With moderate temperatures and precipitation, autumn and spring in southern Ukraine are longer than in steppe regions to the north and east. Crimea enjoys dry, hot summers and mild winters.

• Cities •

About two-thirds of Ukraine's 51.9 million people live in cities. The country has several urban centers with more than a million residents and many medium-sized towns.

Kiev, the Ukrainian capital, is a city of 2.6 million people on the Dnieper River in the north central part of the country. The city's legendary founder, the 7th-century ruler Kyi, built a fortress to protect the site from raids by the nomads of the steppes.

Later, Kiev became a major trading center that linked the Black Sea region with nations and cities in northern Europe.

Kiev was the seat of the earliest Slavic principalities (states ruled by princes), as well as an important religious hub. The **Tatars** of central Asia overran and destroyed the city in the 13th century. Kiev became a possession of the kingdom of Lithuania in the 14th century after the Tatars retreated from eastern Europe. The city was brought into the Russian Empire in the 1600s. During World War II (1939–1945), fighting between German and Soviet forces caused extensive destruction in the city. Nevertheless, many of Kiev's historic churches and public buildings have survived.

Kiev remains an important industrial and communications center, providing a vital transportation hub for Ukraine's farms and factories. Workers in the city produce cameras, precision tools, clothing, aircraft, watches, and chemicals.

Since the 1800s, this square in Kiev has been the site of rallies and demonstrations in favor of Ukrainian independence.

A merchant at Kiev's Bessarabka Market prepares large, locally grown squash for sale. Built in the early 20th century, the covered market presents a selection of produce as well as examples of Ukrainian folk art.

Orthodox services are held in St. Andrew's Church, an 18th-century masterpiece in Kiev. Designed by the Italian architect Bartolomeo Rastrelli, the church stands on the highest point in the oldest part of the capital and has a commanding view of the Dnieper River.

East of Kiev is Kharkov (population 1.6 million), a city settled by the military brotherhood of **Cossacks** in the 17th century. Located near vast fields of coal and iron ore, Kharkov (Kharkiv in Ukrainian) has become the country's chief industrial city. In addition, it is a lively cultural and literary hub with a long tradition of music, theater, and opera.

An important industrial city along the Dnieper River is Dnepropetrovsk (population 1.1 million). This busy river port and railroad junction also has more than 3,300 acres (1,335 hectares) of parks. Mining and metalworking caused the rapid growth of Donetsk (population 1.1 million), an industrial and educational center in southeastern Ukraine. The capital of the Donetsk Oblast (province), Donetsk is part of an extensive mining and industrial region —known as the Donbas—that lies along the lower Dnieper and Donets rivers.

Ukraine's main seaport is Odessa, on the northwestern shore of the Black Sea. More than 100 nationalities make up Odessa's population of 1.1 million. The city's name derives from Odesos, a Greek colony built on the site in the 4th century B.C. A manufacturing and trading center, Odessa is the

Odessa, a large port on the Black Sea, contains more than 100 ethnic groups. An Asian vendor (below) *offers passersby a spicy carrot dish. Boats of all kinds* (bottom) *crowd Odessa's docks, which welcome fleets from many foreign countries.*

In a Lvov park, schoolchildren pass in front of a statue of the Ukrainian writer and journalist Ivan Franko. His works, which appeared in the late 18th and early 19th centuries, include plays, novels, poetry, and literary criticism.

site of a large shipbuilding industry. The first motion picture studio in the Russian Empire was built in Odessa, which still has an active film industry.

Lvov (Lviv in Ukrainian), the principal city in western Ukraine, has a population of 798,000. The Ukrainian king Danylo (Daniel) Romanovych, who built the city in the 13th century, named it after his son Lev. Narrow cobblestone streets and ancient buildings have survived in the Old Lvov neighborhood, which also boasts many parks and cafes. Ivan Franko University, founded in 1661 and named after a famous Ukrainian writer, is one of the oldest universities in Europe. Lvov's railways and roads link the city to the rest of Europe and help Ukrainian companies to ship their goods to foreign markets. Factories in Lvov make machinery, chemicals, heavy vehicles, electrical equipment, and processed food.

(Left) **A descendant of 17th-century Cossacks, or peasant fighters, wears the group's traditional embroidered shirt.** (Right) **A young Slavic girl in Kiev cuddles her black cat.** (Below) **To supplement her food supplies, this woman cultivates a small vegetable patch near her home.**

• Ethnic Heritage and Language •

The population of Ukraine is 51.9 million, of which 37 million are **ethnic Ukrainians.** Ukrainians form the majority in all 25 of the country's oblasts, except in the Crimean Peninsula, where Russians make up the majority. **Ethnic Russians** total about 22 percent of the population of Ukraine. Other ethnic groups include Belarussians and Poles. More than 8 million Ukrainians live in other former Soviet republics and in foreign countries throughout the world.

Rural areas and cities have been steadily growing in this densely populated country for decades. Most of the large cities are in central Ukraine along the Donets and Dnieper rivers. These industrial and mining regions have attracted large numbers of workers from other parts of Ukraine and from

Tatars (above) *and Russians form the majority population on the Crimean Peninsula, where the climate is mild and sunny. A woman in Lvov* (below) *wears the fashionable clothing typical of western European cities.*

other former Soviet republics. Western Ukraine is also heavily populated, but most of its people live in villages and on farms. Many Tatars, who were the first group to settle in the Crimea, have sought to return to this peninsula from their homes in Russia. The mild climate of the Black Sea coast attracts many vacationers as well as new permanent residents from outside Ukraine.

Many of Ukraine's people speak both Ukrainian and Russian. These closely related Slavic languages use slightly different versions of the Cyrillic alphabet. Since the 19th century, Russian leaders have attempted to **Russify** the nation, in part by forcing Ukrainians to use only the Russian language. After the country gained its independence from the Soviet Union, the Ukrainian government promoted the everyday use of Ukrainian.

• *Religion and Holidays* •

The major religion in Ukraine is the Eastern Orthodox faith, a branch of Christianity. Unlike the Roman Catholic Church, which has a single leader in the pope, the Orthodox church is made up of separate, self-governing churches. When Ukraine fell under Russian domination in the 17th century, the Ukrainian Orthodox Church was forced to become part of the Russian church. Until 1990, the only official church in Ukraine was the Russian Orthodox Church. With Ukraine's independence, however, the Ukrainian Orthodox Church has been restored.

Ukrainian Catholics make up the second largest denomination. Catholics recognize the pope as their spiritual leader, but in Ukraine the Orthodox liturgy is used in Catholic services. The Soviets disbanded the Ukrainian Catholic Church in 1946. After operating underground for 44 years, Ukrainian Catholics again gained official recognition. Catholic parishes also serve ethnic Poles and Hungarians. Most Ukrainian Protestants are Evangelical Baptists or Pentecostals.

Several synagogues (Jewish houses of worship) have reopened recently to serve Jewish Ukrainians, who make up about 1 percent of the country's population. Most Ukrainian Muslims inhabit Crimea, where the Islamic Ottoman Empire ruled from the 1400s until the late 18th century.

Ukrainians observe many holidays, including Christmas, Easter, and Epiphany (a commemoration of the baptism of Christ). Church holidays are normally celebrated according to the old Julian calendar, which is 13 days behind the more commonly used Gregorian calendar. As a result, Ukraine's Christmas Day falls on January 7 rather than on December 25. The country's Independence Day is August 24, but Ukrainians also celebrate January 22, the independence day declared by

An elderly Ukrainian prays respectfully at a streetside shrine. After bringing Ukraine into the USSR, the Soviets restricted the practices of the Ukrainian Orthodox Church. As a result, most young Ukrainians have little knowledge of their country's dominant religion.

Ukrainian leaders in 1918. Ukrainians mark civic holidays with religious services and processions. They are also fond of singing and dancing, and many choirs and dance groups participate in holiday events.

Dressed in traditional clothing, women in Pereiaslav-Khmelnytskyi welcome visitors with bread and music.

A Ukrainian Orthodox bishop leads a procession in Lvov. In the 18th century, Russian rulers forced Ukrainians to join the Russian Orthodox Church. The Ukrainian Orthodox Church regained its independence in 1991.

Ukrainian folk dancers perform at a theater in Kiev.

• Education and Health •

The educational system, like many aspects of life in Ukraine, is going through tremendous changes. Under the Russification policy, Russian-language education began in day-care centers and in kindergarten. Teachers were trained by the state to teach the ideas of Communist leaders and historians. Since independence, schools have revised their courses and have reintroduced Ukrainian as the language of the classroom.

Children begin school at age six. They attend four years of elementary school, followed by seven years of secondary school. Education is compulsory through the 9th grade. Students who finish formal schooling may attend a vocational institute to learn a trade. More than 700 technical colleges train workers in job skills.

A mother holds her young child while begging for money and food at a market in Kosov.

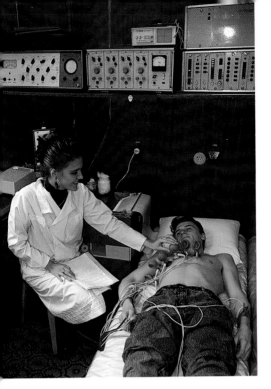

In some urban centers, residents benefit from up-to-date health services. Here, a technician monitors a patient's heartbeat.

Secondary schools, which prepare students for universities, offer a variety of subjects and guide students in independent work. Some secondary schools emphasize a particular area of study, such as English or computer programming. After graduating from secondary school, students must take a competitive exam to gain admission to an institute or university. More than 100 postsecondary schools, including nine universities, operate in Ukraine.

Ukraine has a shortage of medical equipment and modern facilities, especially in rural areas. Nevertheless, the country has achieved a low infant mortality rate—18 deaths for every 1,000 live births. This is lower than the rate in most former Soviet republics. In addition, life expectancy in Ukraine is 71 years, which is also a little better than the average in the old Soviet Union.

Thirteen-year-old students practice speaking English at a school in Lvov.

CHAPTER TWO

Ukraine's Story

E vidence of human activity in Ukraine dates back to 150,000 B.C. The earliest known farmers in Ukraine were the Trypillians (4500–2000 B.C.), who lived in long, rectangular log houses that sheltered a clan of 15 to 20 people. The Trypillians cultivated wheat, barley, millet, and rye and tamed wild horses, sheep, pigs, and cattle.

Between 1000 B.C. and 200 B.C., various nomadic peoples—including Cimmerians, Scythians, and Sarmatians—migrated to the steppes of Ukraine. The Slavs, who originated in eastern Europe, are the direct ancestors of the Ukrainians. Slavic groups moved south to the Black Sea region in the 4th century A.D. to escape the invasions of the Huns from central Asia. By the 6th century A.D., Slavic groups were settling the land near Kiev and creating a new state that would grow into a mighty empire.

Founded by the Kievan prince Yaroslav the Wise in the 11th century, St. Sophia's Cathedral in Kiev has survived foreign attacks and political turmoil.

The legendary founding family of Kiev (left) *are depicted on the prow of a boat in a monument in the capital. A silver coin* (below) *dates from the reign of Prince Volodymyr the Great* (A.D. 980–1015).

• Kievan Rus •

History books known as chronicles describe much of Ukraine's past. In 1113, a Ukrainian monk named Nestor wrote a chronicle describing Prince Kyi and his family—the legendary founders of Kiev—who lived in the 7th century. The new settlement flourished until it fell under the brutal reign of the Khazars, an Asiatic people. In the 9th century, the early Ukrainians invited Askold and Dir, powerful Viking rulers from northern Europe, to govern Kiev.

Although they accepted this invitation, Askold and Dir were later killed by members of the Rurik dynasty (family of rulers). Prince Oleg, the leader of the Rurik dynasty, conquered Kiev in A.D. 882. At that time, Ukrainians were known as the Rus people, and the state established by the Ruriks was called Kievan Rus.

Volodymyr the Great, who lived during the 10th century, was the fourth member of the Rurik dynasty to rule Kievan Rus. Seeking to unify the Slavic peoples of the region, Volodymyr converted to Christianity in 987. He then required all of his subjects

to accept the Christian faith. When Christianity split into the Roman Catholic Church and the Eastern Orthodox Church in the 11th century, the Ukrainian church aligned with the Orthodox faith.

Kiev, the political center of Ukraine, was also a thriving commercial city. The Slavic realm controlled much of the trade between northern Europe and the Byzantine Empire, whose capital—Constantinople—was located to the south in what is now Turkey. The Greek-speaking Byzantine Empire, the center of the Orthodox faith, also influenced the culture, religion, and language of Kievan Rus.

Volodymyr's son and successor, Yaroslav the Wise, developed Kievan Rus by building schools and churches, by establishing written laws, and by promoting the arts. He forged close ties with other nations by marrying his three sons and three daughters into European royal families. By colonizing lands to the north and east, Kievan Rus became the largest state in all of Europe. But after Yaroslav's death, the realm broke into separate principalities that were ruled by his many relatives.

Prince Volodymyr's son Yaroslav (above) *promoted the Christian faith in Ukraine in the 11th century. He also sought to protect and strengthen his domain by building earthen walls around Kiev. The city's walls fell down long ago, but the entryway—called the Golden Gate* (right)—*still stands.*

• *The Galicia-Volhynia Principality* •

The breakup of Kievan Rus left the Slavic state with weakened defenses. The Tatars, skillful warriors from central Asia, invaded eastern Europe in the 13th century. To escape the invaders, many Ukrainians moved westward into the Galicia-Volhynia Principality in what is now western Ukraine. This state remained independent until 1340, when the death of the last Galician prince caused a struggle for control of the region among the powers of eastern Europe. Galicia fell to Poland, and the region of Volhynia became part of Lithuania, a powerful state north of Ukraine.

When Lithuania united with Poland in 1569, these lands and the city of Kiev came under the rule of the Polish king. As subjects of Poland, the Ukrainian people eventually became **serfs**—farm laborers who were the property of landowners. In addition, the Poles introduced the Polish language and attempted to convert Orthodox believers to Roman Catholicism, the faith of the Polish people. In 1596, most of the Ukrainian Orthodox bishops changed their loyalty to the Catholic Church. This action established the Ukrainian Catholic Church.

To fight these changes, the Ukrainians organized brotherhoods that undertook educational and religious work. The brotherhoods began in Lvov and spread to other cities. In addition, a new Ukrainian Orthodox leadership was established in Kiev in 1620. In 1631, the Kievan metropolitan (church

Batu Khan, leader of the Tatars, sacked Kiev in 1240. The destruction of the city forced many people to flee into what is now western Ukraine.

A musician plays the bandura—a traditional stringed instrument that often accompanies Ukrainian folksongs.

In Lvov, a Catholic stops at a small shrine on the grounds of St. George's Cathedral—the center of Ukraine's Catholic Church. While Polish kings ruled Ukraine, Orthodox clergy agreed to accept the authority of the Roman Catholic Church—the church of Poland—without changing the form of the Orthodox liturgy. This decision established the Catholic Church in Ukraine.

leader) Petro Mohyla founded the Kievan Academy, the first Ukrainian institution of higher learning. The 17th century was also marked by great works of Ukrainian literature and a flowering of the arts.

• The Cossacks •

Throughout this stormy period of Ukraine's history, the nation's traditions and culture were defended by a military brotherhood known as the Cossacks. The first Cossacks were former serfs who traveled south to fish and hunt in the dangerous frontier regions of the Ukrainian steppes. In time, they organized a force to challenge the attacks by the Tatars and to resist the harsh rule of the Polish king.

Cossacks were Ukrainian peasants who formed a disciplined fighting force in the 17th and 18th centuries. The dedication of the Cossacks to the Ukrainian Orthodox Church helped to maintain the country's national and religious identity during periods of foreign rule.

This golden cupola, or dome, belongs to the elaborate Monastery of the Caves in Kiev. Founded in the 11th century, the site contains natural caves as well as artificial ones carved by monks living in the monastery. The grounds also hold the graves of Cossacks.

The Cossacks lived a life of freedom yet were a disciplined group that chose its **hetmans** (leaders) in open elections. With their reputation as the best fighting force in Europe, the Cossacks attracted **peasants**, nobles, and even some foreigners to Cossack settlements along the lower Dnieper River. For about 200 years, the Cossacks remained the strongest defenders of the Ukrainian people and of the Ukrainian Orthodox Church.

Although the kings of Poland could do little to control the Cossacks, these rulers needed allies to fight the Tatars and other invaders. The Poles created units of "registered Cossacks," who lived on their own land and who helped the Polish army in time of need. Other Cossacks inhabited fortified settlements and fought for whomever they pleased.

• The Hetmanate •

The harsh conditions suffered by Ukrainians under the Polish kings caused violent uprisings of peasants and Cossacks. The hetman Bohdan Khmelnytskyi led the largest such revolt in 1648. Khmelnytskyi defeated the Poles and created a new state ruled by Cossack leaders. The name *Ukraine,* which had been used for centuries to describe this Slavic borderland, now described the territory of the Cossacks' hetmanate.

A statue of Bohdan Khmelnytskyi shows the Cossack hetman (leader) on horseback carrying a mace (club) that symbolizes his authority. In 1654, Khmelnytskyi freed his people from Polish control by arranging a defensive alliance with Russia. Within a few decades, however, the Cossacks were trying to break free of Russian rule.

As the Poles prepared to counterattack, Khmelnytskyi sought help from the czar of Russia, whose empire lay northeast of Ukraine. In 1654, in exchange for Russian aid, Khmelnytskyi swore an oath of loyalty to the czar and signed the Treaty of Pereiaslav. The Russians believed that the Cossacks had submitted to the czar by signing the treaty. After Khmelnytskyi's death in 1657, Russian leaders sent military forces to Ukraine and appointed a governor to rule the region.

In an attempt to regain its independence, Ukraine allied itself with Poland and Lithuania in 1658 and defeated Russian forces at the Battle of Konotop in 1659. Eight years later, however, Poland and Russia divided Ukraine along the Dnieper River. Russia seized lands to the east of the waterway, and Poland took over territory to the west.

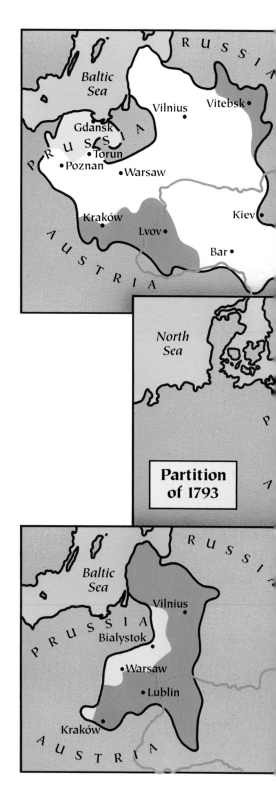

Partition of 1793

In the 1700s, the Cossack hetman Ivan Mazepa sided with King Charles XII of Sweden against Russia. Here, Ivan (right) chats with the king near the site of the Battle of Poltava.

Russian Partitions (late 1700s)

- Polish-Lithuanian Commonwealth
- To Prussia
- To Russia
- To Austria
- Current border of Ukraine

Partition of 1772

Partition of 1795

Baltic Sea
Vilnius
Gdansk
Minsk
Torun
Poznan • Warsaw • Pinsk
Kraków
R U S S I A
T R I A

Miles
0 50 100 200
0 100 200
Kilometers

Maps show progressive partitions (divisions) of territory in eastern Europe by Russia, Austria, and Prussia (northern Germany). By the late 1700s, Russia completely controlled Ukraine.

Several Cossack leaders attempted to regain control of Ukraine. In the early 1700s, Hetman Ivan Mazepa joined forces with King Charles XII of Sweden against Czar Peter I. But the Russians defeated the Swedes and the Cossacks at the Battle of Poltava in 1709. Peter I then used Cossack prisoners as forced labor to build canals and cities in the Russian Empire.

The Cossacks survived as an independent fighting force and continued to resist foreign rule over Ukraine. But the hetmanate could not win against the large, disciplined armies of Russia. In 1775, the Russian empress Catherine II sent her troops to attack the Cossacks. By 1781, the hetmanate had ceased to exist, and Catherine added Ukrainian territory west of the Dnieper River to her realm.

Throughout the 19th century, Russia benefited from Ukraine's productive agriculture and growing industry. To impose Russian culture, the czars passed laws banning the Ukrainian language. In addition, the Russian government forbade the building of churches in the Ukrainian style.

During World War I (1914–1918), revolutionaries called Communists overthrew the Russian government. Ukrainians saw this rebellion as an opportunity to become independent of the Russian Empire. On January 22, 1918, Ukrainian politicians established the Ukrainian National Republic and authorized the use of colorful new currency (above).

• The Ukrainian Republics •

Within the Russian Empire, hunger and poverty caused growing discontent in the early 20th century. In addition, a global conflict was brewing that would pit Russia, France, and Britain against Germany. At the start of World War I (1914–1918), Russian armies suffered defeats at the hands of German forces in Ukraine and in other regions. Revolutionaries known as Communists called for an end to the czar's rule and for the establishment of a new government. Vladimir Lenin, a leading Communist, promised bread, land, and peace to the empire's workers and peasants.

After the Russian Revolution overthrew the czar in March 1917, Ukrainians again sought independence. Ukrainian leaders founded the **Ukrainian National Republic** on January 22, 1918, with Professor Mykhailo Hrushevsky serving as the republic's first president. Several nations—including Lenin's new Communist state—recognized Ukraine's independence.

The Communist regime built a broad archway in Kiev to commemorate the reunification of Russia and Ukraine.

A scholar and historian, Mykhailo Hrushevsky served as the first president of independent Ukraine. The Ukrainian National Republic lasted only until 1921, when the Communist Red Army took over Ukraine's territory and added it to the Union of Soviet Socialist Republics (USSR). After the takeover, Hrushevsky went into exile in Austria but returned to Ukraine in the 1930s. His popular nationalist writings prompted the Soviet government to arrest and confine him in Moscow, the Russian capital city.

In 1918, however, Ukraine became the scene of a devastating civil war between Ukrainians, Poles, Czechs, Communists, and Romanians. Four years of heavy fighting among many factions drove the government of the Ukrainian National Republic into exile. The conflict destroyed Ukrainian cities and brought widespread famine and disease. In the spring of 1921, the Communists finally defeated their opponents. After Poland signed a treaty with Lenin's government, Ukrainian territory was divided among the Communists, Poland, Romania, and Czechoslovakia. The independent Ukrainian republic ceased to exist, and a new government was hastily formed. The major Ukrainian cities, including Kiev, came under the control of the Communist government.

The **Ukrainian Soviet Socialist Republic** became part of the Union of Soviet Socialist Republics (USSR) in 1922. The Ukrainian and Russian republics signed an economic and military union, and Lenin's government stated that Ukraine was an equal partner with Soviet Russia. Although it was one of the founding members of the USSR, Ukraine had little independence.

To gain support in the region, the Soviet government allowed Ukraine to preserve its language and permitted Ukrainian farmers to sell their produce on open markets. But the rapid revival of a Ukrainian independence movement in the mid-1920s alarmed the Soviets. By 1929, the Soviets were

Under Soviet rule, farmers no longer owned the land they farmed. They were required to give their harvest to the state, which then distributed the crops. The central government also combined many small holdings into large estates called collectives.

A survivor of the Ukrainian famine of the early 1930s drew this view of the Soviet effort to force people to accept collectivization. The government seized all food crops in Ukraine, arresting people for taking even small amounts of wheat for their families. As a result, about six million Ukrainians starved to death.

executing writers and artists who opposed Communist rule in Ukraine. In addition, the government of the USSR took over factories, farms, and local governments.

• Industrialization and Famine •

To develop the USSR's economy, the Soviet leader Joseph Stalin ordered new mines and factories to be built in Ukraine in the late 1920s and early 1930s. Stalin also abolished family farms and replaced them with state-run **collectives**, which the government created by seizing and combining small, private plots. Farmers had to give up all their land and animals to the collectives. They became ordinary workers on government-owned estates and were paid with small portions of food produced on the collectives.

Those who did not want to join the collective farms were executed or sent to Siberia, a remote region of Russia. To feed factory workers and to end resistance to collectivization, Stalin ordered the seizure of crops and seed grain. This action by the Soviet government caused millions of Ukrainian peasants to starve to death.

In the late 1930s, a military threat to the Soviet Union emerged in Germany, where Adolf Hitler and the Nazi party had come to power. Although Germany and the Soviet Union signed the **Molotov-Ribbentrop Pact**, which banned conflict between them, the two countries were preparing for war.

• World War II •

Germany broke the treaty by attacking Ukraine and other Soviet territories in the summer of 1941. The Soviet government enlisted Ukrainians to fight Hitler's invading armies. Many Ukrainians, however,

saw the Germans as their liberators from Soviet rule and joined the German forces. Others created an underground army to fight both the Germans and the Soviet Red Army.

In 1945, the war ended with Germany's defeat. The years of conflict had damaged Ukrainian cities, towns, and farms. Eight million people had died, and countless more had either been deported to Germany as slave labor or had fled the Soviet Union. After the war, the Soviet government added territory to Ukraine. Poland surrendered land that is now part of western Ukraine, and Crimea was transferred from Russia to Ukraine in 1954.

In the 1950s and 1960s, the Soviet government ordered Ukrainian weapons factories to begin producing industrial goods. Throughout these decades, busy mines, industries, and farms provided the republic with a strong economy. Huge mills supplied steel for new construction, and collective farms grew enough grain to support the Soviet Union's expanding population. Ukraine became an essential part of the five-year economic plans that guided the USSR's economy.

(Above left) *To slow the German advance into Ukraine during World War II (1939–1945), the Red Army mined the main church of the Monastery of the Caves with explosives.* (Above) *The Babi Yar monument in Kiev commemorates the deaths of nearly 100,000 people, mostly Jews, who were massacred during the German occupation.*

• The Fight for Democracy •

Despite the economic strength of Ukraine, years of mismanagement by the Communist government resulted in a sharp economic decline in the late 1970s and early 1980s. The inefficient system of state-owned factories and farms caused shortages of consumer goods and food. Communist leaders, who sought to keep control over the USSR's economy, resisted nearly all economic reforms.

This situation changed after Soviet president Mikhail Gorbachev, who came to power in 1985, introduced the policies of *glasnost* (openness) and *perestroika* (restructuring). Ukrainians seized the opportunity to revive their traditions and to replace the Russian language with Ukrainian in their schools. In September 1989, Ukrainians created a national democratic group called **Rukh** (meaning "movement" in Ukrainian). In 1990, to protest Soviet control of Ukraine, Rukh organized a human chain. Half a million men, women, and children linked hands

The symbol used by Rukh, the modern Ukrainian independence movement, recalls the image that appears on coins from the time of Prince Volodymyr.

In the early 1990s, Ukrainian flags decorated a snow-covered grave of unknown soldiers who died during World War II.

and stood along a 300-mile (483-km) highway between Kiev and Lvov, marking the unification of
Ukrainian lands in 1919.

In open elections held in March 1990, pro-
democracy candidates won 25 percent of the seats
in the Ukrainian parliament. At the same time, independence movements in other Soviet republics
were threatening to break up the USSR. To prevent
this development, Gorbachev urged the republics
to sign a union treaty. This agreement would have
granted some independence to Ukraine but would
also have reserved important powers for the central Soviet government.

In August 1991, just before Ukraine and other
Soviet republics were to sign the treaty, conservative Communists attempted to overthrow Gorbachev.
Although this coup d'état failed, the Communist party's authority rapidly declined. Ukraine proclaimed
its independence on August 24, 1991. By a public
vote held in December 1991, an overwhelming 90
percent of Ukrainians approved this action.

Leonid Kravchuk, a former Communist party official, became Ukraine's president. Kravchuk also
adopted the program of Rukh, which called for an
independent, democratic Ukraine. On December
25, 1991, Gorbachev resigned, and the Soviet
Union formally ended. Several nations, including
Poland, the United States, and Russia, then recognized Ukraine as an independent country.

• The Future of Ukraine •

Ukraine has moved quickly to set up its own
democratic government. The newly independent
country is also planning to issue a new currency
called the hryvnia. The blue-and-yellow national flag
of Ukraine has replaced the Soviet flag. Although
Ukraine was a founding member of the **United Na-**

tions in the 1940s, it always voted under Soviet direction. Ukrainian representatives now speak for their own country and not for the Soviet Union.

In December 1991, President Kravchuk met with representatives of Russia and Belarus to form the Commonwealth of Independent States. Other former Soviet republics later joined this organization. Nevertheless, Ukraine and Russia still disagree on military and trade policies. The two nations have signed a treaty to divide among them the former Soviet naval force stationed in the Black Sea.

Ukraine's leaders are working to repair the damages of Communist mismanagement. The country has signed a number of international trade agreements, has sold many enterprises to private owners, and has set up a **market economy**. Although Ukraine is undergoing a difficult transition, the country's vast human and natural resources may eventually lead to prosperity.

*(Left) **Ukraine's president Leonid Kravchuk, a former Communist, has struggled to assert his country's independent authority. Along with the presidents of Russia and Belarus, Kravchuk agreed to form the Commonwealth of Independent States as an economic association of former Soviet republics. Conflicts between Ukraine and Russia, however, have made the future of the commonwealth uncertain.** (Below) **Activists demonstrate for freedom and democracy in front of the Ukrainian parliament building.***

In early 1992, the Ukrainian government replaced the ruble, the old Soviet currency, with coupons (above). Only Ukrainian citizens receive the coupons, so that outsiders cannot purchase goods to sell abroad. The coupons will be in use until the hryvnia—Ukraine's new currency—is introduced.

CHAPTER THREE

Making a Living in Ukraine

A s a member of the Soviet Union, Ukraine sent most of its income to the central government in Moscow. Although some of the money returned to the republic, it was not enough to meet the needs of the Ukrainian population. The inefficient and costly system of central management supported a privileged few and caused great hardship for most of Ukraine's people.

A land rich in natural resources, Ukraine supplied 25 percent of the USSR's industrial production, 25 percent of its agriculture, 30 percent of its meat, and 50 percent of its iron ore. Of 64 different products and raw materials exported by the USSR, 46 came from Ukraine.

The Ukrainian government has taken over the mines, farms, and factories on Ukrainian territory that once belonged to the Soviet government.

A farmer sits on a mound of corn, one of Ukraine's main crops.

Ukraine now produces goods for its own needs. Surplus production will be exported, and the profits will remain in Ukraine for future investment.

• Industry •

Ukrainian industry was crucial to the Soviet economy. Ukraine's declaration of independence in late 1991–and the resulting loss of manufactured goods from the region–played a large part in the final breakup of the USSR. Nevertheless, Ukraine and Russia will probably remain trading partners. Both nations produce essential fuel and mineral resources and depend on each other to provide markets for finished industrial goods.

The Donbas region in southeastern Ukraine once furnished more than one-third of the Soviet Union's steel. Coal and iron-ore mines in the area now supply raw materials to plants in Dnepropetrovsk and Donetsk. Factories in these industrial centers produce steel, heavy machinery, chemicals, and agricultural fertilizers.

In the eastern city of Poltava, a worker (above) *monitors machinery that makes giant rotary engines called turbines. A series of tanks* (below) *allows a plant near Donetsk to make agricultural fertilizers and other chemicals.*

UKRAINE'S ECONOMIC ACTIVITIES

Industry		Mixed Livestock	
Textiles		Cereals and Grain	
Shipbuilding		Sugar Beets	
Coal		Potatoes	
Oil		Fruit	
Hydroelectric Energy		Flax	
Nuclear Energy		Tobacco	

When parts are available, new cars roll off this assembly line in northeastern Ukraine.

In the northeastern city of Kharkov, factories make trucks, mining equipment, textiles, and chemicals. Lvov, in western Ukraine, is a hub of textile production. Food-processing industries operate in Kiev and in other northern cities. The smaller hubs of southern Ukraine also have food-processing plants. In Odessa and in several other ports on the Black Sea, shipbuilding and oil refining are important.

A Ukrainian boy watches over his family's cow. Food and meat have become scarce since independence, and livestock are often the targets of robberies.

• Agriculture •

About one-third of Ukraine's land is under cultivation or is used as pasture. Before independence, Ukraine was the most productive agricultural area in the Soviet Union. The government no longer directs the collectives set up under Soviet rule, and Ukraine now encourages private ownership of farms. With a new system of planning and administration, agricultural production should improve in the future.

Farmers raise cereal crops, such as wheat and corn, in central and southern Ukraine. Sugar beets also thrive in these regions. The cooler climate and less fertile soils of the north support potatoes, rye, sunflowers, and flax (a plant used in textile production). In the south, where less rainfall occurs, irrigation projects have helped farmers to cultivate vegetables and to develop fruit orchards. Tobacco and wine grapes grow in the hills of southwestern Ukraine and on the Crimean Peninsula. Livestock raised in Ukraine include cattle, sheep, poultry, and pigs.

Workers gather ripe pears on a collective farm in southern Ukraine (above). *Combines harvest corn near Poltava* (below).

• Mining and Energy •

Ukraine is rich in mineral deposits, and mining has long been an important economic activity in the region. The Donbas area is a major center for the mining of coal and iron ore. Ukraine also has the world's largest deposits of manganese ore, a vital component of steel and cast iron. Factories use Ukrainian titanium to make airplanes, submarines, and heat-resistant glass.

THE LEGACY OF CHERNOBYL

On April 26, 1986, an engineer at the Chernobyl (Chornobyl in Ukrainian) nuclear power station in northern Ukraine watched in amazement as the dials on the control panel began to glow. Moments later, workers reported that an explosion had ripped apart a nuclear reactor at the facility. The blast started more than 30 fires and threw 11 tons (10 metric tons) of **radioactive** particles into the air.

Radiation, which is invisible to the human eye, consists of high-energy rays. When radioactive materials strike an object—like the engineer's control panel—these rays cause the object to give off heat. This scientific fact, when implemented on a large scale, produces energy at nuclear power plants. In high doses, however, radiation also destroys living tissue, causing cancer, birth defects, or even death in people, animals, and plants.

Unwilling to believe that the nuclear reactor was destroyed, the Soviet government did not inform the public of the explosion until almost two days later, when scientists in Sweden detected radiation passing over their country. As a result, about 100,000 people were exposed to deadly levels of radiation before being evacuated to outlying areas.

Five years after the closure of the Chernobyl nuclear power plant, Ukrainian activists (left) pressed for nuclear safeguards. A young victim of the disaster (inset) continues to receive medical treatment for radiation sickness.

The increased radiation in the area has caused thousands of people, especially children, to suffer from cancer, blood diseases, and stomach ailments. Every year, the government sends some young Ukrainians to northern Europe and to the United States for a few months to reduce the levels of radiation in their bodies.

Since the disaster, Ukrainians have held protests against nuclear power plants. Because of these efforts, some completed reactors have never opened, and others in the planning stages have never been built. Nevertheless, reactors at Chernobyl that were not damaged by the explosion are still in operation. The Ukrainian government, however, has ordered the closure of the entire station.

Chernobyl itself is now a ghost town. Houses and trees were bulldozed and buried beneath the contaminated soil. Workers enclosed the destroyed reactor in a steel and cement containment building, but radiation continues to leak from this structure. Most experts doubt that people will ever be able to live in Chernobyl again, and many believe that the consequences of the explosion will still be evident thousands of years from now.

Ukrainian mines produce graphite and many varieties of clay that can be used for pottery, metal casting, soap, textiles, and bricks. Kaolin, another type of clay, is used in ceramics, in medicine, and in aluminum. There are also deposits of marble, gold, gemstones, and semi-precious stones. An almost inexhaustible supply of salt exists in several regions, with some layers more than 600 feet (183 m) thick.

Ukraine's clay deposits are the raw material for this ceramic factory in Lvov, where a worker crafts a new piece of porcelain.

A technician prepares a huge mobile drilling rig for use in a Ukrainian oil field.

Although Ukraine has its own reserves of natural gas, this pipeline brings in additional supplies from Russia.

Ukraine also benefits from extensive energy resources, including natural gas. The country has limited supplies of oil, however, and must import this vital fuel from other former Soviet republics. Dams and artificial lakes run hydroelectric plants that lie along the Dnieper River. Coal-fired plants in the Donbas region provide electricity to nearby factories and mills.

Ukraine has its own supplies of uranium, an element needed in the production of nuclear energy. But the explosion and fire in 1986 at the Chernobyl nuclear plant north of Kiev has raised serious concerns about the future of nuclear power in Ukraine.

CHAPTER FOUR

What's Next for Ukraine?

A market economy—in which businesses can freely produce and sell goods to make profits—is a drastic change for Ukrainians. By allowing private citizens to own and operate businesses, the Ukrainian government has made a break with the Communist system of central planning. The country's economic future now depends on the success of its products in a competitive world market.

An open market, however, means that the government must allow prices to rise. This policy makes it difficult for Ukrainians to buy consumer goods, even though wages in the country have increased. The introduction of the hryvnia—the new Ukrainian currency—may help to stabilize the economy.

Mindful of their history, Ukrainians are sensitive to the actions of the new government in Russia. President Kravchuk has said that Ukraine will act in the interest of its own citizens. Nevertheless, Ukrainians are optimistic that relations with Russia will be friendly and that trade will flourish—since both countries need each other's markets and products.

On the banks of the Dnieper River, Ukrainians gaze at the domes of one of Kiev's many churches.

FAST FACTS ABOUT UKRAINE

Total Population	51.9 million
Ethnic Mixture	73 percent Ukrainian 22 percent Russian 1 percent Belarussian 1 percent Moldovan 1 percent Polish
CAPITAL and Major Cities	KIEV, Kharkov, Lvov, Dnepropetrovsk, Donetsk, Odessa
Major Languages	Ukrainian, Russian
Major Religions	Ukrainian Orthodox, Ukrainian Catholic
Year of inclusion in USSR	1922
Status	Fully independent state; founding member of Commonwealth of Independent States; member of United Nations since 1945 as Ukrainian SSR but changed name to Ukraine in 1992

At a peaceful student demonstration, a young activist wears a hat that says, "For a free Ukraine."

Although Ukrainians are suffering from a weak economy, there is little violence between its ethnic groups. In November 1991, a nationalities congress was held to assure Ukraine's various ethnic groups that they can learn their own languages, teach their own culture, and practice their own religions.

The Ukrainians also have good relations with their neighbors to the west. Hungary and Poland, the first countries to recognize Ukrainian independence, have maintained active trade and cultural ties. Ukrainian diplomats and business owners are traveling to eastern Europe and around the world to attract foreign investments.

Many Ukrainians are asking their legislators to speed the country's needed political and economic reforms. Others, however, fear the country's uncertain economic future and want to return to a planned economy. Although most Ukrainians favor democratic reforms, it may take some time before life improves for the average citizen.

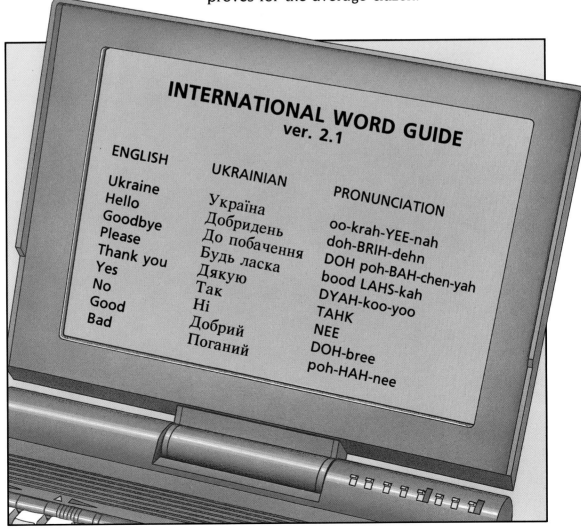

INTERNATIONAL WORD GUIDE
ver. 2.1

ENGLISH	UKRAINIAN	PRONUNCIATION
Ukraine	Україна	oo-krah-YEE-nah
Hello	Добридень	doh-BRIH-dehn
Goodbye	До побачення	DOH poh-BAH-chen-yah
Please	Будь ласка	bood LAHS-kah
Thank you	Дякую	DYAH-koo-yoo
Yes	Так	TAHK
No	Ні	NEE
Good	Добрий	DOH-bree
Bad	Поганий	poh-HAH-nee

chornozem: a rich, fertile, black soil present throughout much of the Ukrainian steppes.

collective: a large agricultural estate worked by a group. The workers usually received a portion of the farm's harvest as wages. On a Soviet collective farm, the central government owned the land, buildings, and machinery.

Commonwealth of Independent States: a union of 11 former Soviet republics that was created by the leaders of Russia, Belarus, and Ukraine in December 1991. The commonwealth has no formal constitution and functions as a loose economic and military association.

Communist: a person who supports Communism —an economic system in which the government owns all farmland and the means of producing goods in factories.

Cossack: a member of a military brotherhood that was first organized by former serfs. The Cossacks lived in the lower Dnieper River valley and fought the rulers of Russia and Poland for Ukrainian independence.

coup d'état: French words meaning "blow to the state" that refer to a swift, sudden overthrow of a government.

ethnic Russian: a person whose ethnic heritage is Slavic and who speaks Russian.

ethnic Ukrainian: a person whose ethnic heritage is Slavic and who speaks Ukrainian.

Snow blankets the rich, black soil, called chornozem, that covers the fertile plains of Ukraine.

Dressed in traditional costumes, ethnic Ukrainians perform at a theater in Kiev.

glasnost: a Russian word meaning "openness" that refers to a policy of easing restrictions on writing and speech.

hetman: one of the elected leaders of the Cossacks, who inhabited territory north of the Black Sea from the mid-17th to the late 18th centuries.

industrialize: to build and modernize factories for the purpose of manufacturing a wide variety of consumer goods and machinery.

market economy: a system that allows the free exchange of goods at prices determined by supply and demand.

Molotov-Ribbentrop Pact: a political agreement negotiated by Vyacheslav Molotov of the Soviet Union and Joachim von Ribbentrop of Germany. Signed in 1939, the agreement said that the two nations would not attack one another or interfere with one another's military and political activities.

peasant: a small landowner or landless farm worker.

perestroika: a policy of economic restructuring introduced in the late 1980s that loosened Soviet control of industry and agriculture.

radiation: energy that is given off in the form of rays or particles. Some rays and particles become **radioactive** as a result of the breaking up of atoms.

Rukh: a political group that favors democratic reforms within Ukraine.

Russian Empire: a large kingdom that covered present-day Russia as well as areas to the west and south. It existed from roughly the mid-1500s to 1917.

Russify: to make Russian by imposing the Russian language and culture on non-Russian peoples.

serf: a rural worker under the feudal landowning system, which tied laborers to a farming estate for life. Serfs had few rights and owed their labor and a large portion of their harvest to the landowner.

Slav: a member of an ethnic group that originated in central Asia and later moved into Russia, Ukraine, and eastern Europe.

steppe: a flat, treeless plain that stretches across central, northern, and eastern Ukraine.

sukhoviyi: hot, dry winds that blow during the summer in Ukraine.

Tatar: a member of the Turkic ethnic group that originated in central Asia.

Ukrainian National Republic: an independent nation formed in 1918, after the Russian Revolution toppled the Russian Empire.

Ukrainian Soviet Socialist Republic: one of the original Soviet republics that was incorporated into the USSR in 1922.

Union of Soviet Socialist Republics (USSR): a large nation in eastern Europe and northern Asia that consisted of 15 member-republics. It existed from 1922 to 1991.

United Nations: an international organization formed after World War II whose primary purpose is to promote world peace through discussion and cooperation.

The Carpathian Mountains are home to this rural Ukrainian.

A Note on Place Names

The spellings of many place names in Ukraine are changing from Russian to Ukrainian. In this edition, we chose to use the spellings that appear on most maps and in most other publications. Listed below in the left column are current names. In the right column are spellings that may soon come into common use.

Bug River	Boh River
Dnepropetrovsk	Dnipropetrovsk
Dnieper River	Dnipro River
Dniester River	Dnister River
Donetsk	Donets'ke
Kharkov	Kharkiv
Kiev	Kyiv
Kosov	Kosiv
Lvov	Lviv

• *Photo Acknowledgments* •

Photographs used courtesy of: pp. 1, 8, 9 (left), 19 (right), 22, (top left, top right, and bottom), 34 (right), 38, 43 (right), 44 (top), 45, 50 (bottom), 53 (inset), 54 (right), 61, 62, Dr. Anatol and Mrs. Daria Lysyj; pp. 2, 5, 11 (bottom), 16, 17 (left and right), 18, 19 (left), 21, 23 (bottom), 27 (top and bottom), 31 (right), 33 (left), 35, 39 (right), 40 (left), 43 (left), 46, 60, Jeff Greenberg; pp. 6, 9 (right), 10, 11 (top), 20 (bottom), 25 (top), 30 (left), 42 (right), 44 (bottom), 48 (top), 51 (bottom), 52, 56, Tania D'Avignon; p. 13, © Dennis Noonan; pp. 20 (top), 23 (top), © Yury Tatarinov; pp. 24, 26 (bottom), 33 (right), 58, Bohdan Hodiak; p. 25, Slavko Nowytski; p. 26 (top), © Eugene G. Schulz; pp. 28–29, M. Eugene Gilliom; pp. 30 (top right and bottom right), 39 (left), 42 (left), Ukrainian Museum, New York, New York; pp. 31 (left), 48 (bottom), 50 (top), 54 (left), 55, TASS / SOVFOTO; p. 32, Independent Picture Service; p. 34 (left), Library of Congress; p. 36, Saporetti; p. 41, Mykhailo Ivanchenko; p. 51 (top), © Tom Caples. Maps and charts: pp. 14–15, 48, J. Michael Roy; pp. 36–37, 58, 59, Laura Westlund.

Covers: (Front) © Eugene G. Schulz; (Back) Dr. Anatol and Mrs. Daria Lysyj.